Power of Me

Discover the Future

Keith Timewell

authorHOUSE®

AuthorHouse™ UK
1663 Liberty Drive
Bloomington, IN 47403 USA
www.authorhouse.co.uk
Phone: UK TFN: 0800 0148641 (Toll Free inside the UK)
*   UK Local: 02036 956322 (+44 20 3695 6322 from outside the UK)*

Published by AuthorHouse 09/04/2020

ISBN: 978-1-7283-5666-2 (sc)
ISBN: 978-1-7283-5475-0 (hc)
ISBN: 978-1-7283-5665-5 (e)

Print information available on the last page.

This book is printed on acid-free paper.

To my beautiful wife, Alice,
And to my Al-anon family and friends group
Special thanks to
Paula Gee & Sarah Jane McIntyre.

CONTENTS

FOREWORD

I have known Keith my whole life, he's my uncle. The evolution of Keith has been an extremely unique and interesting journey to watch and to play a small part in.

As a child, my brother and I would spend summer holidays with Alice and Keith, our glamorous aunt and uncle. We'd be flown down to London, our small town selves already dizzy with the anticipation of what adventures lay ahead of us.

It was the 1980s and we could not believe our luck! We were taken to dinner in five star hotels, shopping sprees for toys in Hamleys and day trips we will remember our whole lives - Windsor Castle, Thorpe Park, Madame Tussauds, racing through the Surrey countryside in open topped sports cars. We loved every thrilling second.

This window into another world continued well into the 1990s. As an awkward teenager, Keith gave me a summer job working in his hotel near Newcastle, my confidence went through the roof. Auntie Alice booked me a hair appointment at a top salon, Keith arranged for a stretch limousine to pick us up and drive us to the Theatre Royal. By the time we were on the flight back to Glasgow, our suitcases packed with brand new wardrobes, the idea of our usual everyday existence already felt like a bit of a comedown.

Keith was a workaholic. He didn't switch off and seemed to be working twenty-four hours a day hence his success, wealth and the lifestyle which my brother and I were privileged enough to experience.

However, what goes up must come down, and eventually Keith came down. He was unable to continue working in the hotel industry and his health issues stopped him from working again.

There was another side to Keith. Keith has always had a calmness about him, an ability to engage anyone in conversation and give them valuable advice. He has always been a "people person", he is interested in what's going on in your life as well as how you are feeling.

In this book, *Power Of Me,* Keith is imparting his knowledge and view of the world to the reader. This is a person who has experienced material success and discovered that it was meaningless without being true to who you really are. Regardless of your political or religious beliefs, Keith speaks to the reader and guides you to improve your life by discovering just how powerful each of us really is.

SJ McIntyre   May 2020

FLY - First Love Yourself is a wonderful principle. Learning to put it into practice is easier said than done.

Those of us who have addictive natures have two problems: before and after we achieve abstinence. In advance our arrogance knows no bounds. We believe the world has problems and we have solutions. In retrospect we recognise we had this the wrong way round.

Keith Timewell is clear that we need to love ourselves just enough to be ourselves. And love means the absence of judgement. As he says, 'no amount of shame, guilt, hurt or debts is worth wasting a life'.

He, along with Albert Ellis in Rational Emotive Behaviour Therapy (REBT). and Aaron Beck in Cognitive Behavioural Therapy (CBT) argues that changing our thinking changes our life for the better. But Keith Timewell goes further. He shows that action is what makes all the difference.

Modesty - and amusingly accurately - he says that if we struggle with technology, we should ask a five-year-old. In other words, consult someone whose head is not cluttered up with previous beliefs and experiences.

In Power of Me, we are shown - step by faltering step through interactive reading experience - how to make the changes in our lives that he has dramatically made in his.

Dr Robert Lefever
Founding Director and Counselling Trainer of one of the first rehabs in the U.K.

CHAPTER 1

FLY Without Wings

In this modern world of perfectionism or chaos, people are driven by greed, EGO, 'Empty God Out', pride, and lack of love for themselves. The focus on material things, vanity, or the fear of failure may cause them to internalise these feelings and emotions.

Kindly take my advice, as I learnt how to change my thinking. I am pleased to share my thoughts and a lot of physical, mental and spiritual pain. Take what you like and leave the rest.

To understand *'The Power of Me'* will require a mind-shift and changing your core beliefs and principles. Your journey of self-discovery begins with your action *now*. Find out who you really are, because you are a worthwhile person: the resident expert of any job is the person doing the job now.

Changing the core principles of the self-belief systems of your own life will be the most challenging thing you will do, but also the most rewarding. Turn your thinking around, be honest, face the truth about yourself, and stop hiding behind the fake mask you wear to cover your pain and brokenness.

There is no worse pain than beating yourself up because you're afraid of what will happen to friends and family if you told the truth. *Love* yourself enough just to be yourself. Internalising those emotions and feelings is not the solution, it's just covering up the problems with life. FEAR is False Evidence Appearing Real.

Love is probably the most misused word worldwide.

But what is this love stuff?

Love means the absence of judgement.

Phil Schofield, the well-known TV presenter, could no longer stand keeping his secret of twenty-seven years and came out to the nation on live television. With the strength of living in the now, he just did it. He stopped overanalysing and faced the truth. Pain can be too much for some people to live with, and they succeed only in wasting their own lives rather than coming out and facing their fears.

No amount of shame, guilt, hurt, or debts is worth

wasting a life. With *"The Power of Me"*, you will cherish every moment today. Sadly, there's no easy solution or quick fix, but absolutely no situation is ever worth dying for. There is always a solution. Help and support are there. It's hard, but it's time to put up your hand and ask for help. You need never stop asking. Then you can move from living in DENIAL, to loving yourself enough to embrace the 'Power of *You*'.

Change your thinking, and you will change your life for the better. Don't live in fear or DENIAL for twenty-years as Phil Schofield did, projecting guilt, shame, and a fear of what people would think of him. When he did come out, there was nothing but respect, love, and acceptance. So, remember this: 95 per cent of what you worry about never happens. You die if you worry, and you die if you don't. You are a worthwhile human being. Never prejudge people by their looks, it's truly what's inside that counts.

You are the resident expert of you. No matter what others may think or say, what *you* think of yourself is what counts. Love yourself enough just to be you, and what other people think about you is none of your concern.

In developing 'The Power of Me', I learned that if you want to be someone, try being yourself first. Be kind and respectful. It works for you if you work for it. Start your journey of self-discovery. Now that you've bought the book, use it and get value for your money. Kindly take my advice, as I'm not using it today. Have a happy life living in 'HOPE'.

When you choose to change your thinking, all will be in your hands. Then you will move from *'The Power of Me'* to the *'Power of You'*, with a life free of the past and of anxiety for the future.

Throughout this book you'll be encouraged to take control of your life by changing your core beliefs. Changing your thinking will change your life from living in DENIAL to living in HOPE; happy, joyful, and free to be yourself, probably as you have never lived before.

Remember when you were a child? You were born with one emotion: love for your parents or caregivers, who, if you were privileged, could not do enough to keep you safe. You were 100 per cent honest. Sadly, in adult society, people are at best less than honest and bend the truth. But children today are not stupid. If as an adult you struggle with technology, ask a five-year-old, and they'll tell you what to do.

In this modern world of chaos and information overload, most businesses are slow to come around to embracing change and investing in people in balance with technology. People too often struggle with life, with physical, emotional, and mental issues. Bosses need to care more and sack less. They are not surrounded by idiots. We are all equals. There is no such person as a bad employee, just bad employers and teachers.

Your future is now. Stop thinking and just do it. People who say *"Let me think about it"* have no intention of changing their thinking. They may die never having experienced a happy life, only the HOPE of one. Change your should, in to must. Actions speak louder than thoughts.

"How can I FLY without wings?" you may be thinking. To *FLY* is to *'First Love Yourself'*. Traditional thinking would have you living life with all the outdated limitations of your parents' thinking. Only if you can have an open mind and heart will you stop thinking and start to love and respect yourself enough. It is better to beg for forgiveness than ask for permission, sometimes.

Start your journey of self-discovery now. Evaluate the core principles that have shaped your life, good or bad. These may need a few alterations or updating to meet the changes demanded for your future, 2020 and beyond, question everything, how you think can stop you from achieving.

To start, you'll need to learn to *FLY 'First Love Yourself'*. That is, put a little love in everything you do, because you can't serve from an empty bowl. You can't give away something you haven't got inside: your love and respect for yourself and others.

Learning to *FLY* is the first step in the right direction, which is better than using 2,020 to step in the wrong direction. Don't think about it too much, because your mind will tell you that you can't do it. To *FLY* is not to listen to others' opinions. The key to your happiness is in *your* pocket, not anyone else's.

Remember, *FLY, 'First Love Yourself'*, to empower yourself and let go of your past. Stop being anxious about a future that doesn't exist; your future is now. For it is not where you have been that matters, what counts is where you are going. Start to live in the now, dream big, and stop thinking about it, just do it. You'll be amazed with the results. Put your needs first, lose the people-pleasing mask, and start looking after you. *'The Power of Me'* is a tool to help you unlock your true talent, connect to your inner self, and move from feeling powerless to looking in the mirror and saying, "I have *'The Power of Me'*."

FLY without Wings

Commitment of Action

Stop Doing	Start Doing

∽ ❀ ∽

CHAPTER 2

Declutter Your Life

The busy pace of life today, information overload, chaos, crisis after crisis in 2020 and beyond, all this is now set to move even faster. But remember, the key to your happiness is in your pocket. No amount of material wealth will make you happy. Money is just a tool. *'The Power of Me'* brings a life experience of HOPE, strength and happiness, which you will maybe find helpful. What is vital to success is in short supply and priceless: your time. Time is precious, waste it wisely or accept the consequences. First you need to learn to embrace your brokenness.

Stop trying to please everyone and exhausting yourself. You'll never please other people or meet their needs, so start putting *you* first. Don't say no in a selfish way, just respect and love yourself enough to say no in a caring way. Remember no is not a word you need to justify.

You will need the full strength of your mental health to stop thinking about it and just go on the journey. Begin now with that one step in the right direction rather than 2,019 steps in the wrong direction. Just go for it.

One suggestion for a change of thinking? Decluttering. Begin to declutter the shame, guilt, and feeling of worthlessness you may have wasted time on. Try dreaming big, and you will achieve more in your life that you could imagine.

Embrace change instead of living in the past or trying to understand everything that may bring happiness in your future. Your future is now, so start to live. 95 per cent of what you worry about will not happen, so why waste time worrying? Start cherishing every moment, walk through the seasons, see the beauty of nature, and start to refocus for life. Love what makes you happy, no matter what everyone else wants. Your needs come first.

Don't accept other people's bad behaviour and attitudes toward you. Let go of resentments, for they are a complete waste of your time. Holding resentment is like drinking poison and expecting someone else to die. The only person you're hurting is yourself.

Instead, heal people with your words, expressed with love and not your anger or hatred. Changing your thinking and core principles will not be easy, it is rather like trying to turn a battleship around in a bathtub. You don't need to remember how much of your time could have been spent on what pleased you or how your relationships may have benefitted.

Self-love means respecting yourself too, using the single word no or yes said with meaning. It is your choice what you remember, and your needs come first.

Everyone is aging, some more quickly than others. Are you making the most of your mental, physical and spiritual growth by exercising, eating a good diet, and changing your thinking? Or are you so busy pleasing others that you are too exhausted, flaked out on the couch in front of the 62-inch TV to escape your complicated life? Maybe having a drink or two to relax after a stressful time at work, struggling to get the kids to bed and walk the dog before it gets too dark?

Working hard to please others is a balance of your time. You are worth more, and you'll pay the price in more than the value. Is your lifestyle a treadmill of work, sleep and no exercise? That will affect your health. Some people think they know best, does that sound like you? Confused by now? Just remember by loving yourself enough, to be you, is not selfish, it's just self-caring. To do the next right thing, sometimes may not be exactly right for you at that moment in time. Just be kind. Choose what your heart believes. You'll be amazed when you change your thinking, it will reward you with more time and money to invest in yourself, plus, you'll start to feel younger, less stressed and pressure will fade away. With the

'Power of Me', you'll grow with love and respect for yourself and move from being powerless, to the *'Power of You'*.

Wellbeing is the new buzzword. What does it mean? Every day that you love yourself, changing your core principles will result in you taking back your life. You'll have more quality time to have fun with your family, you can have a long lie in, go to the park, or market and buy the things you want.

In the past you gave every piece of your mind to other people but changing your thinking means; looking at whether you are spending your hard-earned money to please others? Do you only think you want it for an image or the vanity of feeling good? Ask yourself, do I really need all this to clutter up my house? It may be nice to have, but is it needed? Why not try only for a week, to not spend what you have not got. Start to love what you have got, not what you think you want. You'll be happier and have the money to buy what you need without the pressure of having spent what you didn't have. Let go of addictions; drinking, drug taking, shopping, gambling, smoking and so many other things that damage your health and cost you more than just money. A major mind shift of your thinking is required, or Monday comes along again with no growth. The damage of failing to change your thinking will lead to putting your health at risk, until you have a heart attack and die. All because you have been living in DENIAL, unwilling to listen to your doctor's advice.

How many times have you thought about decluttering, but never got around to doing it? You are digging a hole, first stop digging, then start doing what you need to do. You'll be glad you have more time, money and an amazing peace of mind in your life. Take your doctor's advice, life is precious, waste it wisely. Cherish every moment, laugh a lot, have fun, review your lifestyle, review your habits, understand the harm alcohol, smoking and habit-forming drugs can do to your wellbeing. The faster pace of life will speed up stress, with the advent of 5G some people may struggle even more, so this chapter is dedicated to giving them some tools and suggestions to what may add value if they apply them.

No life problems are worth dying for. There are generally solutions to every problem. The hardest thing to do is to stop worrying, overthinking and blaming others. Let go of the chitter chatter in your head, put your hand up and ask for help. Be honest, stop hiding behind fake illnesses. You may have to accept that failure is an option, a great lesson is to accept your own accountability, check out the help on offer at the back of this book.

Move your life forward, don't stand still worrying, you'll die if you worry and you'll die if you don't. Stop worrying, you're worth it. Be happy, today will never return. Cherish people, places and things, there are people waiting for you to ask for help. Have a happy life free of negative thinking, what other people may think of you is none of your business, you are powerless to change their thinking. The only opinion that matters is yours. No one else is qualified to judge you. You are the resident expert on you so start decluttering your life now.

'Change and Grow'

Humility is the ability to give up your Pride and still retain your Dignity

Hope ♥ Intouch

Declutter for Life

Commitment of Action

Stop Doing	Start Doing

CHAPTER 3

People First

I am saddened by the abuse of customers in 2020 UK, Service in some businesses is an optional extra, if at all. After 48 years as a hotel general manager, starting with a castle hotel in Glenborrodale, Scotland, with 27 bedrooms, to my last hotel, with 159 bedrooms in Newcastle, I know what good service looks like and how to deliver it, without demotivating employees or exploiting customers. After retiring from many years in hospitality I am horrified to witness how much the leadership has changed. The focus on the cutback of products and services, reduced customer service and paying higher prices for poor service. Has no one else seen this sad change to all industries? It is clear there is a major switch from investing in people, to, regardless of product and services, investing too much in technology. Prices are rising, whilst workforces are being diminished and executives are getting richer. Employees are being pressured with increased workloads, without training support and clear directions from weak leaderships. They are all paying the consequences for the lack of investing in people. Ill health, breakup of families, suicide and mental health issues. All of these things damage the NHS, with a very high proportion of their patients directly due to drug and alcohol related illnesses.

Staff attitudes reflect their treatment from the top. Managers are given zero empowerment, this results in 70% of employees seeking employment elsewhere, because of weak leadership, with the boss making millions of pounds in bonuses.

Training development of effective leadership has reached an unacceptable low. There is no magic wand to change this. No lessons are being learnt from books like 'The One Minute Manager', 'Thriving on Chaos', 'The Joy of Stress' even current books like 'Surrounded by idiots: The Effective study of Human Behaviour'. Lifelong learning is vital to keep up to date. Once leaders get that high paid job, they don't listen to others who have done the job before them, they just think they need to cut back costs, regardless of staff, and they will start to pay the consequences.

After all that is said you cannot build a house on sand. A good business must first start with a strong foundation, based on putting people first, balanced with the right technology to support the product. Reduce costs, increase sales and make more profit, ask Sir Richard Branson or Sarah Willingham or many other successful leaders who are expanding their market share. Not so in the hospitality industry customers are being overcharged and receiving a poor service. In general, industries are not price sensitive, using higher prices to cover inefficiencies.

After a successful career, and as a manager, I am horrified with the way people are being abused in the workplace. The consequence of this is that it rolls out into the home, causing break ups and people turning to drink and drugs. With the unhappiness of employees who have no support or help, domestic violence, suicide and mental health issues increase daily.

The situation originates from fear of economic insecurities, and this is often caused by people's ego, greed, bad attitude and wrong choice of words at senior level. A recent book titled 'Surrounded by idiots', is a good example of how to understand communications of attitudes and behaviour. The definition of communications is to create understanding, but today's communication creates misunderstanding and confusion. The communicator believes themselves to be in control, but the reality is that the listener has full control of what they hear, which is not necessarily the message being relayed. There are some businesses who invest in quality training, care for their employees' mental and physical health and they are the ones with strong leadership who have total empowerment.

The time is now to make a change in management behaviour, attitudes and thinking and a shift in people's leadership, from turning a blind eye to peoples' issues, to 'how can I help you'. In the late 1970's a book was written called 'The One-Minute Manager', detailing a highly successful strategy which has grown into an international training company. The current bestselling international book, has the title *'Surrounded by Idiots: The Four Types of Human Behaviour'*, a change in thinking from the normal tradition. Ramping up communication skills, applying an understanding of human relationships, stopping mental abuse, applying a 'can I help you' attitude. Life in *DENIAL* is, *'Doesn't Everyone Notice I am Lying'*? People in *DENIAL* are lying to themselves and others, as they don't accept that they have any problems, and therefore they don't think they need to change. Placing people first is a difficult concept for most people to grasp.

Bosses thinking that they are surrounded by idiots is abysmal. No one is an idiot. There is no such person as an idiot, just poorly led people, due to poor communication, this together with little awareness of the power of human relationships, empowerment, trust and better understanding. More openness with the *'triangle of power'* being turned upside down, and you accounting for your own judgement and actions.

We are all here to change the world, not just to follow rules, earn money and deny responsibility for abusing the community. How can we change the situation?

Sticks and stones can break you bones, but names will never hurt you. This is wrong today, with social media, where abuse, hatred and put downs destroy people's self-worth, breaking people with mental health issues, driving people insane. Many people turn to drink, drugs and other addictions, to cope with their life problems. This leads them into addiction and mental health issues. This in turn results in pressure on the NHS spiralling out of control. Their workload is driven by mental health related issues and these can lead to serious physical health and subsequently death.

You should be held to account for your words causing wounds not to heal. Senior managers must accept that their choice of words is a statement of their behaviour. If they hurt people, they are contributing to their businesses failing. Their greed, fear of losing what they have and fear of losing their job make them attack as a strategy, blaming everyone else for their own failure.

There are those who thrive on chaos by crushing other people, places and things. All because they can play with people's emotions. They play the blame game, often looking for someone to use as a scapegoat, mentally breaking them with guilt. You can destroy a person with just a poor choice of words. This is currently being repeated across all industries but especially in the hospitality business. This is costing billions in recruitment, training and sickness. Pressurising and trapping employers with as many as 70% of employees seeking to leave their jobs as big businesses rule by fear and intimidation.

Governments and industries are focussing on people's weaknesses, not putting people first, (employees and customers), but in fact, last, as shown by the diagram eg human nature vs human relationship.

Some employer's behaviour is akin to a terrorist, taking hostages with continuous harassment in the workplace. This often leads to similar behaviours transferring to the home.

Hurt people, hurt people!

Children are being scarred by name calling. Lives are being ruined leading to self-abuse and addiction in later life. People who are mentally or physically abused learn distorted behaviour, from bad parenting, to information overload. Our thinking is distorted with too much information and knowledge. Unless you apply this knowledge in life it results in people going to university, only to leave with mental health issues and a degree for which there are no jobs.

There a serious mental health crisis building, with the

increase in young people committing suicide, especially now in the male population. The poor choice of words and lack of support in the community have resulted from government cut backs. They waste millions on projects that take from the weak, like the broken 'universal credit' system, the school syllabus, which is out of date with what children need and what industries require in the future. Teenagers who are bored with education retreat to their bedroom and start up their own businesses. There is no encouragement to be entrepreneurs as there is in America where they support them. The UK needs to wake up and stop their traditional thinking and start to use the talents of their best people, who will ultimately leave the UK for a country that *will* support them.

Most people are being controlled by fear, afraid to use their initiative. This is because when they start a new job, they are not properly trained in what is expected of them. They are not expected to think for themselves, this may explain why so few businesses are thriving. In these exciting times, a business that empowers workers will benefit with a growing market share, like McDonalds, who match the needs of customers by strong leadership, unlike companies like M&S who think their traditional ways are still working, and are closing branches and struggling.

Balancing the future needs of the customer is the sole responsibility of the managing directors. Who need to run two businesses, one is the future and the other is the present.

They need to match the now to be able to meet the future. This is an accountability that they cannot delegate. The employees pay the price and lose their jobs. The anxiety level that the employees suffered with the weak leadership of Thomas Cook is a perfect example that the management wasn't identifying the future needs of customers, however the management still got a golden handshake! They were alright but their ex-employees were not so lucky.

2020 will see more businesses fail as a result of traditional thinking, as well as the Covid-19 pandemic. This prevents the necessity for executives to embrace change. They need to listen to the customers and employees and put other people's needs first. They believe that they are right and no one else's opinions have any value. This is great news for the consultant trade, whose pockets are full of weak leaders. They mistakenly feel that employees are to blame, not the managers. Unlike in sports where football managers are blamed for the team's failure. If this was to be applied for all leaders, where they are held accountable and the buck stops with them, we would all be the winners.

There are three effective factors of management; goal setting; praising and reprimanding, and these will influence people more effectively.

Modern culture celebrates the bold, the brave and the beautiful people that can love themselves enough to be themselves, in this crazy changing world. Where children have the advantage over adults, is that most children are born 100% honest and want to be loved unconditionally. They only learn other behaviour from adults and their peers.

Most adults lie to themselves 85% of the time out of a fear of failure, usually because they cannot love themselves. People pleasing drains them of self-worth and respect, which leads to obsessions and abuse. We need to change core principles and values which for some businesses is like trying to turn a battleship around in a bathtub. Accepting things that can't be changed and changing the things that can, will make an immediate difference in attitude, of 'how can I help you grow?' Growth may be slow but it will be better than standing still.

When Boris Johnson was 5 years old, he made the decision to become Prime Minister. He never stopped planning his strategy to achieve this goal, that led him to achieving his success. Modern thinking and being able to think outside the box have led to him being misunderstood. However now more than ever he is coming into his own.

You need to move your thinking from Living in 'DENIAL', accept your brokenness and start living in 'HOPE'. It's a great mindset to have, you can do it, you're worth it.

The eyes are useless when the mind is blind.

Hope ♥ Intouch

<u>People First?</u>

What behaviour and attitude changes do you need to make?

Stop Doing	Start Doing

CHAPTER 4

Thriving on Chaos

Being honest in 2020 is a bit like trying to empty the sea with a teaspoon, not a winning situation, but I never give up trying. Living with dyslexia is like being trapped inside your own head in silence, controlled by fear that people will not accept you. When you talk to busy people, they understand you, when normal people don't get it they reject you, call you names and abuse your intelligence, believing that they are better than you. People who are dyslexic think differently. They think outside the box. Currently GC Headquarters are actively employing people with dyslexia, ADHD and Asperger's. It's time to change, which people are sought after today.

Dyslexics can be highly intelligent and gifted, with

talented thinking outside of the box, unlike other people who are brilliant academically, they are taught a process, to focus thinking in straight lines on a project until they finish. They are successful because they will not accept failure and will go back to the drawing board and try again. They master never admitting their failures and will blame someone else for their own mistakes.

Dyslexics embrace failure and always have a thousand ideas that no else has ever thought of, they thrive on chaos. They just keep on going, because you learn more from failure than from success. It just needs contemplation and perseverance. This can make other people looking for a scapegoat blame them and they will sacrifice them just to make themselves feel good. If you fail then you have to go back to the beginning and rethink, then follow the process through again. We, dyslexics, live our lives full of ideas, but, afraid to speak, as very few people understand us, or, even have enough patience to hear what we're trying to say.

The world's big problem is communication and creating clarity, you need to assume that people only hear 75% of your message, missing a vital 25%. Today we are living with technology that can send a message around the world in 9 seconds and we are becoming quicker at everything, with 5G becoming available soon. But it can take a lifetime for thought to travel from the head to the heart, a distance of only 9 inches, and to gain acceptance and understanding in your heart, because the person sending it has no control over the listener. They may have prejudices, beliefs, emotions, differences of opinions and this usually ends up creating misunderstandings. We live in an age of information overload.

Many years ago, I let go of my Reality Belief. Running my life my way like most people, I was full of greed and EGO, *Empty God Out*, this was influenced by father's way of anger and bullying, do it my way or the highway. Just thinking about that makes, me emotional, back then it was encouraged to seek money and material wealth. If you're angry you can't be grateful.

Today my life is so different. I reconnected via my Reality Belief, with the love, understanding and support of my family and friends and was able to be myself. My life is so full of HOPE for these exciting times that I am happier than at any other time in my life, with freedom from economic insecurity and pressure of business life, I work for a wonderful boss now, myself.

Today I live with the Joy of Stress. Thanks to my faith, my wife of 45 years and thousands of friends worldwide, I am able to write this book, which I never, even in my wildest dreams, could've attempted. Hence the title: '*The Power of Me*'.

God warning, you may want to skip this bit, the biggest question about God, in my understanding, is not that of the Bible or even a religious belief, is, why does he let bad things happen to good people. Do you think it is to redress the balance from when he lets the good things happen to bad people? The world is in chaos and confusion, largely resulting from an imbalance, where greed and ego are given executive control by fear and bullying tactics. Where only the rich are getting richer as a consequence of the weak.

I used to live in DENIAL. My wife still does. It was like I was on a ladder; everyone was either above me: to be feared and envied, they had what I strived for; or below me, to be pitied. My God was way at the top, beyond reach or understanding. Life was hard, I could not embrace my brokenness, I was lonely and no one could understand me.

No two people can stand on one rung comfortably for long. Then through the Quakers I reconnected with the God who I believe is not religious, just spiritual. My God, Good orderly direction, has given me the courage to change and embrace my imperfections, helping me move into 'Living in HOPE', Help Other People Evolve. With a little help from being united with my lovely wife and support of family and a large number of friends, my life is free of depression, financial insecurity, I am not alone. Their love and help have turned my life around.

The greatest teacher in my world is the God of my understanding. Sadly, you have to open your mind and heart before you can hear other people's experiences, the actual power of communication is not the person sending the message but the courage to invite him in, as he never goes where he is not wanted.

The second greatest teacher in my life is my wife of 45 years. She has taught me to love myself enough and appreciate other people, places and things, or it was my choice to live in isolation. Which do you want to start doing? "My thoughts, I realise, are my head's way of telling my mind lies". My strength is to be kind and live free of criticizing, condemning and judging others and myself which was hurting more people than a bullet. Don't shoot yourself by hurting others.

Sam Walton, just a man with a vision in 1962, set up his first Walmart store. Even when it was a well-established store, he would hundreds of miles every evening to visit competitors' stores, he then would implement some of their ideas in his own stores. He grew his business but he was advised to go public in 1970, due to lack of resources. He had 51 stores by 1972, and, at the time of his death in 1992, Walmart had 1,928 stores and 371,000 employees. Sam Thrived on Chaos which was the motivation he needed to grow his business. His passion, to provide great service at affordable prices, gave him the determination and drive to be able to ignore business advice from others. His belief in himself and his ideas have made his company the richest in the world. He achieved all this by being focussed on his own beliefs and rejecting other people's opinions that his vison would not work. He achieved the impossible with his passion and mental energy. He said

'Outstanding leaders go out of their way to boost the self-esteem of their personnel. If people believe in themselves, it's amazing what they can accomplish.'

Today my strategy is that it is easier to beg for forgiveness, than to ask for permission.
Your only limitation is you!

How do you
communication

T is it true
H is it helpful
I is it inspiring
N is it necessary
K is it kind

Hope ♥ Intouch

<u>Thriving on Chaos</u>

What do you need to change?

Stop Doing	Start Doing

CHAPTER 5

Embrace Your Brokenness

There are only two types of people in this world, people who live in *DENIAL, Doesn't Everyone Notice I Am Lying,* and those who Live in *HOPE, Help Other People Evolve.*

The first type lies to themselves and to everyone else. They never say sorry or accept their mistakes as a learning aid. They are always right. They may have a big house, nice car and everything looks fine, but they're so unhappy inside. They're trapped by success, not able to make any mistakes, if they are asked for help, they will always say, 'what's in it for me?' They are failures as they have no fulfilment in their own lives.

The second type live in *HOPE.* It requires a huge mind shift to move from DENIAL, to Living in *HOPE.* It's like living in a different world, full of optimism, promise and the joy of helping other people evolve. There are a lot of books already written on changing your thinking. Living in *HOPE* is being happy and loving what you've got, not what you may think you want to keep up with your neighbour or friend. You have an independent mind full of love for yourself and others. You can't serve soup from an empty bowl. If you hate yourself, it makes you depressed and discontented with your life. Of course, everyone has bad days, but those that Live in *HOPE* judge the level and don't let it spoil the day that can nearly always be turned around.

People who live in *HOPE* accept their failures as acceptable learning. Their life is fulfilled, happy, joyous and free of stress, depression. Those who worship money never experience true happiness, their success only makes them greedy for more. These people have fake friends and they don't experience their true self. They usually bully their way to control others by fear. They are sad people who are often cash rich but time poor. People who Live in *HOPE* live *cash poor, but time rich* lives, having none of the fear that they're going to lose what they have got.

Happiness is an inside job. No one can make you happy or sad without your permission. Changing your attitude and behaviour is no small task. This book will help you to discover who you really are. Forget about the past, you are not able to change it. Stop worrying about tomorrow, it will only make you anxious. Become a today person, living in the now. Remember you'll die if you worry and you'll die if you don't, so why worry? *HOPE* people have no fear or worry, just freedom to be their true self, happy, joyous and free. For you to change, be warned, there is no quick fix, nor easy solution. Everything takes time which you cannot buy, or get more of. Time is a precious commodity, waste it wisely! There will be no second chance to relive your life. Embrace your brokenness, whether you are fat, thin, rich or poor it is worth loving yourself enough to be your true self. Nobody can do what you can when you connect with your inner self. First love yourself enough to change. Use this book as a tool to help you along a journey to *HOPE* and just be yourself. Stand up for your beliefs or you'll fall for anything. When you embrace your brokenness *'The Power of Me'* will become *'The Power of You'*.

Use the sheet after each chapter, for your commitment and courage to what you will stop and what you are going to start doing. This will help you map out how you're going to change. There is a self-evaluation of the *'3 circles for life'*, from chapter 9, at the back of this book, which are designed to help you through every step of your life change. Use the website, listen to people who made the change and overcame their brokenness, or use the *'Personal Touch Directory of HOPE and Support'* recommended both in the book and with direct links to websites on *'HOPE in Touch'*.

To love life is not an endurance test to survive! Cherish every moment, you're worth it!

There is no job that is not worth doing badly first. You'll learn faster from failure, than you will from being right or from being successful all the time. Nothing happens unless you measure growth. If you have no growth, you're standing still, with no visions or dream of where or what you want to be.

Change and grow.

Start today with life-long learning. There are so many books, tapes, videos, and podcasts, have you been keeping yourself updated? Are there occasions since you left school or university that you seek help? A world of knowledge is available today through many forms of media. Pushing yourself outside of your comfort zone is very hard work, but immensely rewarding and healing as I have discovered and am sharing with you.

The key to embracing your brokenness, is first, awareness. You can't start until you are aware of your weakness or failings. These can then become a strength, when you accept that you have a failing to embrace. Then the real magic will give you the understanding that you can take action necessary for change.

I lived all my life in DENIAL that my dyslexia was not

a problem, by hiding it with coping mechanisms, it became a fact of my life. I would hide my imperfection, because of the shame, guilt and embarrassment that society has created.

Only today by creating awareness that I suffer from dyslexia have I accepted it, and in writing this book it is me taking action. Taking action to embrace my imperfectness with the courage to ask people for help. This is something I have never been able to do. To put up my hand and ask for help was seen by me as failure. The operation to write a book has been the hardest challenge of my life, but so healing and most rewarding. Turning my weakness into a strength was such a surprise, but a feeling of triumph over my shame, what a wonderful experience, I HOPE I can help you too, to turn your weaknesses to strengths.

Henry Fraser, a promising rugby player from the Saracens academy, had a freak accident on a beach in Portugal and was paralysed from the neck down. He never gave up. His determination and changing his thinking. His story can be read in his second book 'Power in You'. This is a testimony to the power of positive thinking. Without question he is *Living in Hope*. He has painted pictures in the finest detail with his mouth, a true *Embracing of his Brokenness*.

Never ever give up on life or your self-belief. Love yourself enough to be yourself, you're worth it. Henry's books are a testimony to that.

Paradigm mindshift will set you Free to just be Your ♥ self

Hope ♥ Intouch

Embrace your Brokenness

What does this mean for you?

Stop Doing	Start Doing

CHAPTER 6

Courage to Change

We are privileged to be alive today, when technology can transmit a message around the world in 9 seconds. It can take some people a lifetime to change and Covid-19 may have destroyed some people's lives and a lot of businesses, but our mind is still our best tool. By acceptance, most people are living with information overload, with social media and the press, radio, tv advertising, and magazines, with more demands on people's time being the result. The definition of communications is to create understanding; however, I believe in 2020 that we have created more misunderstanding, whereby people switch off and are not interested in the message, or they believe everything they see and hear on the internet. Traditional marketing no longer works, most people are immune to the messages. New innovative ideas are needed to fill the marketing gap.

Today we're drowning in words, information overload, demands for our attention from multimedia and advertisements trying to get us to spend money. This creates confusion. Our mind somehow needs to love what we already have so that we are able to only buy what we need. In this fast-paced economy. you need to ask yourself, 'do I really need that?' If not, stop spending, treat yourself with a life experience that will create a memory, be kind to yourself and others, start focusing on your needs in a self-caring way and stop impulsive buying to fill an emotional hole within yourself.

Shopping, overeating, gambling, abuse of alcohol, drugs and sex, co- dependence and many other addictions are all our efforts to block out the acceptance of living on life's terms. People, places and things are just the way they need to be and you are powerless to force solutions. In view of the harm done by the abuse of alcohol, tobacco and other mind changing substances, maybe consider whether you should stop using and start accepting people, places and things just as they are. The use of the drug of your choice will lead to impaired judgment and damage and cause hurt to people around you. "You'll die if you worry and you'll die if you don't' so why worry? Accept your limitations and love yourself enough to be yourself. The time to change is now! The world is changing and your thinking and perception of it must change too.

With the pace of life set to become even faster, it is time to evaluate your thinking and core beliefs. Changed thinking will change your life. Try balancing by measuring your growth via my 3 circles for life self-evaluation you'll find at the end of the book. Life is for living not just existing, start your journey of change by thinking and using the personal touch commitment sheet to record for yourself, what you are going to stop and start doing.

Move out of *DENIAL* and self-doubt, to a new way of thinking. We are all here to make the world a better place to live in, not to destroy it with abuse, of the things around us, or ourselves. You are not here to follow rules and procedures, earn money and continue to live having never discovered your true self. The future is now! There are no problems worth dying for, there are solutions for almost every problem, but it's hard to do. First you must put your hand up and ask for help. Swallow your pride, talk to someone, ask for help, they will not know you need help unless you ask for it, it is there waiting. Stop thinking of the worst and start thinking about how good you'll feel with the direction and guidance out there waiting for you. Seek the solution at the back of this book where there are a few recommended contacts, or go to the '*HOPE in Touch*' website and listen to the podcasts for inspiration and connect to the links to the support you may need. Life is worth living on purpose, to be happy, joyous and free of worry, a day at a time, because you're worth it, just stop thinking about it and do it.

Thinking that you're surrounded by idiots, that you're right and everyone that doesn't agree with you is an idiot is wrong. We all think differently, no two people can ever think the same. What a boring world it would be if they did. So, accept that everyone's opinions are theirs, in a caring way and stop trying to force them to agree with you. This will eliminate your stress levels and you may, by listening to others, learn something. Being right all the time is boring and hurts other people. For it is your poor choice of words that hurt and wound others, destroy lives and devalue people. Your words are your signature. Think what effect you have on your friends, family and colleagues. Happy people will help you to be happy too, hurt people only hurt other people.

Try to live a simple life. Stop trying to be right, start listening. A simplified lifestyle will empower you to enjoy life, surrounded by friends who love you. Remember that strangers are just friends you have not met yet. Talk to people, don't push them away to live in isolation. People are the solutions to all your problems, live the solutions and stopping managing the problem in isolation, you will reduce your stress. Try to compliment people not judge them.

We don't own the world; the chaos is man-made, and it's riches are not ours to dispose of at will. Show loving consideration for all creatures and places, and seek to maintain the beauty and variety of this wonderful world we live in. Rejoice in the splendour of nature, treasure it and stop abusing it. Respect yourself and respect the world we are so privileged to live in. First, love yourself enough, to give love and respect.

Only you can want to make a difference, so go *MAD, Make A Difference*, and care for yourself. If you want to be someone, try being yourself first. Stand up for what you believe in or you'll do anything for a peaceful life. You can make a difference, by showing respect, having ethical values, stop being a sheep and giving your power away to others. Take back your power and just be yourself because you're worth it.

We can approach old age with courage and HOPE born out of changed core values. As far as possible, make arrangements for continuing to care for yourself and respect for family and friends. Don't be unduly a burden to others, whilst times are good, value them, you're a long time dead, so cherish every moment. Live and let live, although ageing may bring increasing disabilities and even loneliness, it is your time to live in the solutions. Be happy to share your experiences, get involved, help others to help too. Always be polite, accept your brokenness and have fun. Laughter is music to your soul, this will bring serenity, detachment, HOPE and wisdom. Don't be bitter about life, live in the solutions just because you can.

Whilst big businesses are getting bigger by control

and takeovers of smaller businesses, the small and starter businesses who are empowered, with passion, innovation and enthusiasm will start to take advantage of, and embrace, the slow reaction to the changes in 2020.

There are only two types of people, those who live in *DENIAL* who lie to themselves and everyone else, this stops them from embracing change, keeping them trapped with their out of date beliefs and fear of failure. And those who live in HOPE, who embrace change and learn from their failures. They reduce all fear of failure, stress and anxiety. Helping others makes them feel good and results in them thinking less about themselves and more about others, as shown by the diagram below.

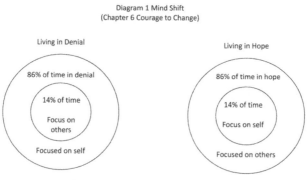

Diagram 1 Mind Shift
(Chapter 6 Courage to Change)

Living in Denial

86% of time in denial

14% of time

Focus on others

Focused on self

Living in Hope

86% of time in hope

14% of time

Focus on self

Focused on others

Changing thinking is key to future happiness, not easy to do. Practice, practice and there will be degree before you will achieve the mind shift.

It takes
Courage to Change
but
It's hard to do

Hope 🧡 Intouch

__Courage to Change__

What do you need to change?

Stop Doing	Start Doing

Mindfulness

Your mental health is the focus in this chapter, looking at the solution rather than managing the problem. All my life I have experienced people at various levels of mental health or character types. It has been my experience that if you have a problem in life, it's usually about first becoming aware, then acceptance and then the final action. Sometimes it is not what you think about that matters, it is what you do that counts, actions speak louder than words.

We are privileged to live in a world with a technological revolution, just like steam did in Victorian times, changes in other life and industry will radically change the world as we know it. So, it will be vital that people embrace the changes and invest in people supported by technology.

Mindfulness covers emotional intelligence and human relationships. If you put in the legwork you too will make a mind shift and start to be yourself, more honest and transparent. By embracing changes, you will achieve your true potential. Nobody needs to die, having had no experience of their own talents, or discovery of their true self.

There are only two characters in life, those who choose to live in *DENIAL, Doesn't Everyone Notice I Am Lying*, and those who live in *HOPE, Help Other People Evolve*, at the risk of repeating this point, by understanding it you will be increasing your awareness. You can then accept and take action, to change your dated thinking. This is the start of a mindful step in the right direction. This is better than standing still in your comfort zone and not changing your outdated values or core principles. Those who Live in *HOPE*, have changed their thinking and core principles, turned their life around and can embrace change. They cherish every moment, happy, joyous and free of the past they live in the now.

Throughout this book, I suggest you take my advice, because I don't need it, I am already *Living in HOPE*, cherishing every moment. I can't wait to get up to the start of a new day, ready to help others with a little of the love and the encouragement I give to everyone. I know this makes me feel good about myself, I no longer have to make excuses, lie to cover my shame, guilt and can embrace my own weaknesses as a strength today. I have no need to over analyse my life in great detail, and never do anything about it. I take the necessary action, stop thinking about it, just do it and accept failure as a learning tool to success. Today I can accept the consequences for my own actions.

Others who are never wrong and use the sandwich technique of shaming and blaming others, have never learnt. This breeds arrogance and contempt, believing that they are somehow better than the rest of us. I pity them, as clearly, they don't love themselves and usually they are emotionally crippled and so full of fear, anger and resentment that they will blame anyone other than themselves.

Emotional intelligence is all about making a difference in the way we think, but first you need to love yourself not in a selfish way but in a respectfully caring way.

This is a true story, a Japanese gentleman of 4ft 4 in got on the underground, the where is not important, he noted in another carriage a drunken man 6ft 6 in tall was threatening the other passengers, swearing and physically abusing them. He got up and walked over to the man and spoke in a calm, soft voice. He said to this giant of a man, 'tell me why you are so angry' to which the man replied, 'it's none of your damn business', so the little man reached up and held out his hand saying, 'let's sit down and you tell me about it' this calmed the man. He sat down and said that his wife had left him and taken his children. He was devastated and was drinking to forget his guilt and shame of the way he had treated her. After a long chat, the Japanese man assured him that things would be different tomorrow. The drink was not helping him. Now the giant man was calm, changing his thinking from poor me, to, I can change, and care more for me. As the little man had said, first love yourself, then give or share. They parted calmly, everyone else was amazed at how the little Japanese man had stopped the unmanageable man's abuse.

This is an example of emotional intelligence applied wisely, but you can't serve soup from an empty bowl. First, love yourself.

Applying human relationships as below is changing your thinking from human nature to human relationships.

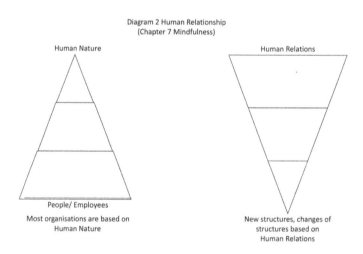

Diagram 2 Human Relationship
(Chapter 7 Mindfulness)

Human Nature

People/ Employees
Most organisations are based on
Human Nature

Human Relations

New structures, changes of
structures based on
Human Relations

You can change from living in *DENIAL* by changing your traditional thinking, letting go of out of date taboo values and principles, to Living in *HOPE,* where you first love yourself enough to be you. Rich people don't fear failure, they learn from keeping an open mind and heart. This will take you from *'The Power of Me' to 'The Power of You'.* Giving you the freedom to own your own life, freedom to use time wisely and stop wasting your life, it is precious, so waste it wisely.

From	To
Live Life in DENIAL	Live Life in HOPE

Your potential is limitless discover it by just changing your thinking

Hope 🤍 Intouch

Mindfullness

What do you need to change to achieve this?

Stop Doing	Start Doing

CHAPTER 8

The Art of Happiness

Remember when you were a child with no responsibilities, just learning through play and listening back. We are all born with 100% honesty. We discover everything about life through play, fun laughter and love with your family, friends and school. We learn to be happy, joyous and free. Sadly, not all children grow up with a loving family. I didn't, I was physically and mentally abused. I dismissed my childhood as just a strict upbringing, because of my dyslexia I was bullied at school as well. Then as we grow up we learn that other people lie, sometimes to hide the truth, and sometimes to protect us and then that honesty and innocence is lost.

Adults manipulate children, they then sometimes let them down with empty promises. Today children are smarter than their parents and can see right through the lies, but they are still powerless as this learned behaviour limits them in future life.

We as adults have lost the art of play and how to be happy, often resulting in poor work / life balance. You learn by first failing, however the world demands perfection, so this impairs your judgement. This stops you from trying to learn, especially as they're playing catch up to their children's knowledge of technology.

When I was 5 years old there were no mobile phones. Although we lived in Llandudno, North Wales, which is a great place to play, it was sad as there was no love or acceptance. In the summer holiday as both our parents were running a small hotel, we as children were expected to be seen and not heard. To suit our parents, my siblings and I were sent to a farm. I would cry and get lost, wondering what I had done wrong. Why was I being punched and sent away, although my sister tried to comfort me it has damaged me.

Children today play with computers not conkers. They are not allowed to play in the street. Parents confuse material things as a substitute for love, so that children need more expensive toys and games. This is especially true when both parents are working. Their feelings of guilt confuse love with material objects. Nothing is as priceless as giving your time. Time spent with them is often denied, damaging the relationship with the parent. It's so easy to make excuses for the lack of support that they are emotionally unavailable to give.

Discovering the art of happiness is to have adventures with your children, creating memories, which is the greatest gift you can give to a child. You need to make the time to play with them. Most adults have no work / life balance, they are often driven by ego and greed for material wealth and they justify it and, they convince themselves, that it is for their family.

This can explain the lack of respect in teenagers. Especially now as they are running wild wilfully. The education process is out of date for 2020. Schools are failing to identify early enough when a child has special needs like dyslexia. Children are bored with the system of education which needs updating, as do some of the teachers.

This is a true story: a young boy's father died and his now single parent mother struggled with alcohol. The boy loved his mother very much but at school because his clothes were shabby and he smelt a bit the other children picked on him. He sat in the front row, he was struggling to read or write.

The teacher decided she would help him. She gave him extra teaching after class and the boy began to learn. Just before the summer holidays, his beloved mother died and he was taken into an orphanage. He continued to attend the same school. At Christmas he wrapped his mother's favourite bracelet, with half the stones missing, and a half bottle of her perfume in a newspaper and gave it to his teacher with a label which said 'You are the best teacher I ever had. Thank you for caring.'

The teacher selected this present despite all the other smartly wrapped presents she had. She told the boy that she would wear them with pride. This made the boy very happy because the perfume reminded him of home and of his mother. He passed his A levels and entrance exams to a top university and sent a card to the teacher. It read 'Thank you. You are still the best teacher I ever had'. This made the teacher happy because she had become a better teacher herself because she had unlocked the talent, he had within him.

The boy thrived in university and passed his degree with honours. He met the most beautiful girl and arranged to marry her. He then wrote a letter to the teacher saying 'You're still the best teacher I ever had and would you like to attend my wedding in place of my late mother'. She of course said yes, as she was so proud of him.

That boy became one of the richest business men in the world and he wrote a letter to his teacher saying 'You're still the greatest teacher in the world. Here are the keys to your new home. Thank you for making me feel special'. Today the teacher every year receives a card saying 'You're still the best teacher in the world to me, thank you for caring'.

That teacher is now the Dean of a top university thanks to

that boy's struggle. She took time to help him, which helped her become a better teacher herself.

That is the true art of happiness, working by caring for other people. Both of them stopped living in *DENIAL* and start Living in HOPE, Helping Other People Evolve.

What is the first thing you do when you wake up in the morning? Are you grateful for a new day? Do you tell your brain to make you happy today? Your brain is programmed to apply your thought sand make them happen. If you wake up feeling unhappy, that is your brain repeating the misery of yesterday, and you will be miserable all day.

The most important thing that you must ask yourself is 'What do I want to change?' In your mind the question must change from 'What is the worst thing that can happen?' to 'What is the best outcome?' Stop giving all your mind space to everyone else, take your control back and focus it on you. Tell yourself that you are a worthwhile and lovable person and you will live a fulfilled life, happy, peaceful and stress free.

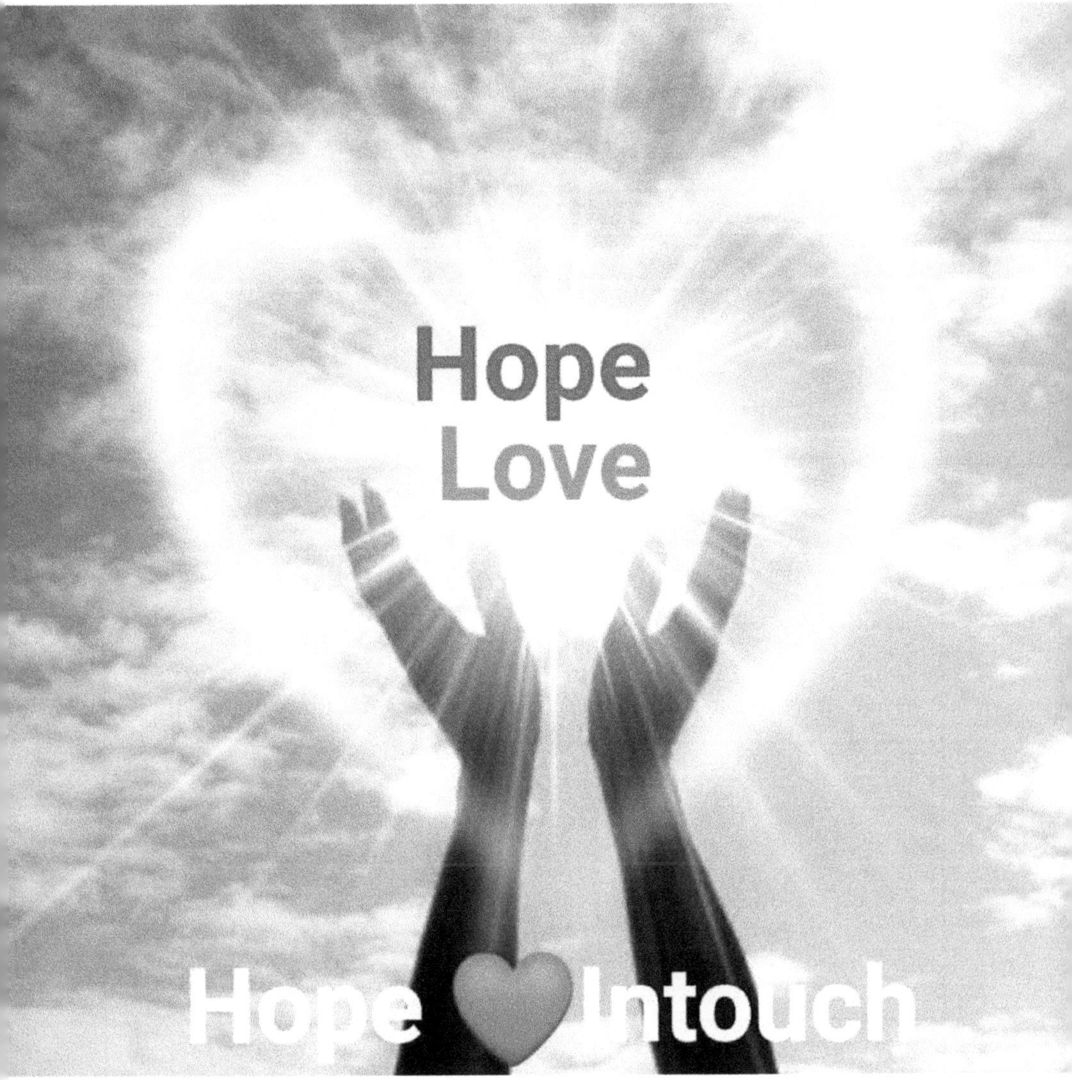
Hope
Love
Hope Intouch

<u>The Art of Happiness</u>

What do you need to do to achieve this?

Stop Doing	Start Doing

CHAPTER 9

Wellness

The 3 Circles for Life

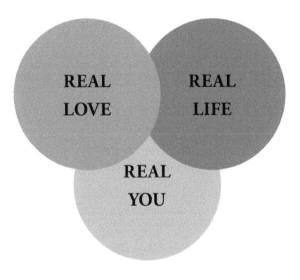

Blue Circle, Real Love

Love is to live with the "absence of judgement" either for others or yourself. Remember you are a lovable worthy person and you learn by doing it, not by just thinking about it. Don't be afraid of growth being slow, be afraid of standing still.

Take better care of your needs first. A little light exercise is better than over doing it. You can see if a person exercises 2 or 3 times a week, it will show in their body. Honesty to make a commitment and stick to it is the difference between thinking and action.

Time is the most important commodity in the world, waste it wisely. Hocus pocus keeps the focus on you. Stop pleasing others and depriving yourself of the love and respect for you. You're worth it.

DENIAL is a word that can destroy many people who HOPE for a better life, only you can make the changes in your lifestyle, by making small changes to your daily routine, regular food and exercise as a bridge to a healthy life with love and respect for yourself.

Love yourself and don't let life make you nervous. It's a bit like a circus animal being let loose with the cage door left open. It takes time to set yourself free. Just take the opportunity, and don't waste time worrying. Our only concern should be our own behaviour and attitudes. Take the small steps towards freedom and care for your own life needs. Take care of your right to live in the now. Taking one step in the right direction is better than a thousand in the wrong direction.

Try reducing your portion size, stop being tricked into eating to please other people. Just eat what you need, don't be afraid to leave food on the plate, it's better there than eating too much and abusing your body. Healthy eating is your responsibility, no one else's. Visualise achievement of your target weight and you will put the footwork in. You need to say, 'no thanks', to that extra portion or to more food than you need. You'll soon be amazed how well it is doing for you and you'll start to feel great.

This is how I personally lost 13 stone. I woke up one morning and decided that was enough. I created change in my thinking, no more overeating to please others. All I needed was just 3 small meals that could fit in the palm of my hand. This is a good guide to portion size. Because life is for the living not existing with hatred and failure in your heart and an unhealthy lifestyle. Today I feel grateful, happy and healthier. My diabetes is in remission plus my sleep apnoea too, I wake up every day with happiness for a new day's adventure.

Breakfast like a king, lunch like a prince and eat dinner like a pauper. Never eat after 8pm. Remember breakfast is the most important meal of the day, get up a half hour earlier, if you have to, to enjoy breakfast, eat slowly, never skip it as it will affect you all day. Eating healthily is loving yourself enough to care for you in a self-caring way, that no one else can do.

Set a target goal for weight and enjoy the mind shift. Ask yourself this question, it may be nice to have cake or biscuits, but, do you love yourself enough to say no. You don't need it. You're worth more than killing yourself with the wrong foods. Thinking just this once will not hurt, yes it will, your thinking will quickly return to bad habits. Just say no and you'll feel so much better.

Red circle, Real Life

A routine to exercise and eating healthily in real terms, will pay off in the long term. There is no quick fix, no easy solution, just the *'Power of You'* and the mind shift within you. You can do it. I managed it and I live in the real world, stop beating yourself up and stop listening to other people's opinions. It is your responsibility to be accountable for your own life. Try expressing your feelings and your concerns, talk to people, join a self-help group, like overeaters anonymous, or any fellowship groups will be helpful, to share those internalised feelings and emotions that often we eat on.

Speak to your doctor, who can help you, but never forget it is your problem. Stop blaming and shaming other people for it. Do it for yourself. Tell yourself that you are a worthwhile, lovable person, not a fat or stupid person. Believe in yourself, as in reality you're just a sick person trying to get well.

My solution was to start living in the now and to do it. Stop being a tomorrow person, become a now person. Live in the present, you learn how to stop thinking about your past history, you can't change it, everyone starts the day with a fresh 24 hours, don't waste a second, because, you're worth it.

Stop being anxious, worrying about the future, and living in the past, it has gone never to return. Just cherish the now, the reality is today and remember you die if you worry and you die if you don't, so why worry, embrace change.

Life is a journey of self-discovery. To find your true self happiness is an inside job. No one can make you sad or happy without your permission. Stand up for yourself or you'll fall for everything, hold onto your values. If you want to be someone, try being yourself first. Be true to yourself, there's no one else like you, you have a special talent that as a result of fear of failure, you have never tried to create. Just change.

Yellow circle, Real You

There is no one as unique as you, maybe you already realise that, or have you been brought up to believe that you must put other people first. There really are no two people capable of thinking alike. All my life, I have always tried to please others before myself, especially in the hospitality trade.

How do you start to put your needs first above others? There's no easy option, it requires a lot of practice, you'll never achieve perfection until you start using the word no. Say no and mean it, only saying yes when it's right enough for you.

People who know you well will question your decision. Stand by your judgement. How many times in the past have you been manipulated into doing something just to please others at your own expense. Remember you can't learn from being right all the time, learn from your mistakes. Life is a great adventure, enjoy every moment just being your real self.

'Not everything that is faced can be changed, but nothing can be changed until you are ready to face it.'

You will die
If you worry
And
You'll die if you
don't
So why worry
it will not
make you feel
better

Hope ♡ Intouch

<u>Wellness</u>

How will you achieve this?

Stop Doing	Start Doing

CHAPTER 10

Applying your Core Principles

Having travelled a great distance in mind mapping to get here, it is time to change your core beliefs, that no longer apply, and need updating along with your core principles. Remember that as a child when you learnt to ride a bike you fell off a few times and maybe hurt yourself, but you got back on the bike and mastered it. Resetting your revamped core principles is vital to the rest of your life, especially if you are aged between 21 years old and death. You'll live longer, feel better and love yourself, allowing yourself to be who you've always wanted to be and free to take back your life.

Life is precious, waste it wisely, you're worth it. Take time to stop wearing the people pleasing mask you have on and try a new way of thinking. Let go of the old ways that you're used to, now help others, not by taking away their accountability, but by keeping the focus on your own needs, first accepting your own accountability.

Applying the three circles for life may be difficult at first but like everything you start doing for the first-time practice, practice, practice, will help solve your problems. Failure only takes place when you give up.

Now by applying the knowledge learned in this book, it becomes 'The Power of You'. When you identify your growth, you'll take back your power that you had given to everyone else. You'll have the choice to keep the focus on you, by measuring yourself by your growth, via the circles for your life, daily, weekly, monthly or yearly. It has to be your responsibility. The sizes of the circles are proportional to your life. The growth may be slow, but it is better than standing still. When you change something, you'll be surprised how much you change. One step in the right direction is better than 2,019 steps in the wrong direction.

By getting honest with yourself, draw the circles to the size of how you feel at that moment in time. Then you can identify where to focus your thinking on a particular area of your life. Your life needs attention to focus in that direction, stop beating yourself up, remember you now love and respect yourself first, placing your needs above others. Never forget you have choices now to say yes or no. That's your right when you let go of trying to please others and focus on you.

There's more to life than just earning lots of money. Keep to the decision that made you dislike life and living in *DENIAL*. Your future is now going forward, with love in your heart. Give it in every step of your new way of thinking. You have moved into a wonderful world of Living in *HOPE*, into the light of happiness, every day you have the *'Power of You'*.

Stop holding on to traditional thinking and resentment of your past, today you may find those values, principles and beliefs out of date, stopping you from living a happy life and eliminating your chance of success. Resentment will kill, as hatred destroys lives. Let it go, with forgiveness, not for those who hurt you, just for the freedom and acceptance to move on. Without the past resentments controlling your life, you'll be free of anger, shame and hatred.

There's more to live for in life than crisis, complaining or condemning people, places or things, obeying the rules, earning money or wounding people with a bad choice of words. You should give a little love to everyone. If you do that, it will surprise you, how other people react to you. You will change too, you can't give what you have not got inside, if you struggle to love yourself, remember, you can't serve from an empty bowl.

Having a belief in yourself, a faith in someone, something or some place is important to embracing change.

A woman on a beautiful spring morning was walking through the forest enjoying smelling the scent of the wild flowers, when she heard a voice in the distance. As it got closer it sounded like a child's voice, she continued to a clearing where she saw a small boy sitting on a stone. She couldn't make sense of what he was saying, he was reciting the alphabet over and over again. She asked what he was doing, the boy replied 'I'm saying my prayers but I don't understand the words but I know that the higher power will understand what I want to say by selecting the words from my alphabet.' She was amazed at his wisdom at such a young age and his belief in something other than just living in his own head, a belief in others is a great way of embracing change.

We all have the choice to make changes in our thinking and accept life on life's terms, by changes to our principle and beliefs, to stop limiting ourselves with out of date thinking from our past, which is no longer successful in this world of great change.

Legends tell of a spiritual journey, in which the hero/heroine must face great challenges before gaining the treasure at the journey's end. Your journey is just beginning. *Living in HOPE* in the now, means despite your life having had, dark times and moments of joy, this will be one of the most important moments in your life, self-discovery of who you are. My RB, Reality Belief, I realise, after accepting support and love from my friends and family, is exploring your hidden motives, secrets, memories and your unrecognised talent, which is sometimes buried deep within. You'll learn to revisit your core values and principles, making huge changes, learning to overcome obstacles and achieving personal growth. Nothing happens if you don't measure your growth using the 3 circles for life in chapter 9.

Only by facing the darkness could I receive the treasure that I now enjoy. The light and joy of emerging on my journey, released me from all of my emotional baggage that had been holding me back.

Self-knowledge is the pathway to freedom. The world is changing fast, I know that my mind-shift will see me through every challenge in the future. Your journey will only progress by accepting your small achievements along the way. My journey has no end yet, I have received so much treasure in my life by *'Living in HOPE'*, and I hope you will too.

Good Luck and remember that there is help available for you in The HOPE Directory on the website Hopeintouch.

Reality
Believe

Hope ♥ Intouch

Power of You

When you get what you want in your struggle for life
and the world makes you a hero for a day,
just go to the mirror and look at yourself
and see what that person has to say.

For it isn't your father, mother, family or friends
whose judgement that matters to you most of all,
the fellow whose verdict counts most in your life,
is that person staring back from that mirror.

You may be like a Jack the lad,
so full of yourself and think you're a wonderful guy,
obsessed with your looks and body fitness.
But that one in the mirror says you're only a bum
if you can't look yourself straight in the eyes

The Guy to please - never mind all the rest,
for its yourself and your thoughts who
will be with you to the end.
You've passed your most dangerous and difficult test
if that person in mirror becomes a friend
and you can love yourself enough just to be yourself.

You may fool the whole world, along your journey in life
over the years and get plenty of pats on the back,
but your final reward will be heartache, illness of health
and may be emotional and tears
if you've cheated on that person in the mirror.
Change or Repeat

<u>Applying your Core Principles</u>

What do you need to change?

Stop Doing	Start Doing

Nothing Changes unless it is Measured

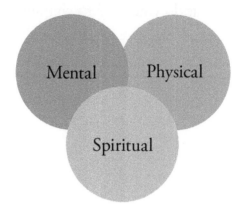

Draw these 3 circles to the size that
you see them at the moment.

Time and Date	
Time and Date	
Time and Date	

Looking back through the changes that you need to make, add them to this Change Summary.

Stop Doing	Start Doing

IN CONCLUSION

This book is designed to help you to create a mind shift, a profound change in the way you think and behave.

You can improve your life and relationships for the better.

This is an interactive reading experience, use the personal touch sheets at the end of each chapter to make a personal commitment to end unwanted behaviours and habits and develop new, positive ways to spend your time.

Over the ten chapters you will create a bespoke guide to help you navigate the journey to a new, improved version of yourself and positively change your behaviour, attitude and thinking.

There is a massive change happening throughout the world as a result of the darkest time in our living history. The world can never change back to the way it was; we need to change to meet the future.

Power Of Me is only a tool, but when you combine it with your own commitment to update and improve your mindset and practices, this will make your world a better place to live in.

We can all carry a message of HOPE, along our journey of self-discovery to reveal who we truly are, these mind shifts are necessary. Stop living in DENIAL and start living in HOPE.

Each chapter shares my experiences while providing strength and HOPE, by applying a unique formula designed to monitor :

- **Growth** - 3 circles for life, for a journey of continuous improvement, to ultimately change your life.
- **Thinking** - A switch from thinking, *"What is the worst thing that could happen?"* to," what *is the best thing that could happen?"*

You can't live a positive life with a negative mind, so it is your choice.

Start living in HOPE. Every chapter has been written to empower you during these difficult times - let go of your fears and anxieties and have love, respect and appreciation for yourself and others.

This will give you the freedom to discover the person you always wanted to be.

Start living in HOPE now. Take back your own life by becoming... the 'Power of You'.

Keith Timewell
Email: hope.in.touch1@gmail.com

Lightning Source UK Ltd.
Milton Keynes UK
UKHW011826310322
400911UK00001B/63